10·00

This 1987 edition published by Derrydale Books,
Distributed by Crown Publishers, Inc.,
225 Park Avenue South, New York, New York 10003.
Printed in DDR.

ISBN 0-517-63365-5

The Twelve Days of Christmas

Illustrated by Cathie Shuttleworth

DERRYDALE BOOKS
NEW YORK

On the first day of Christmas,
My true love sent to me
A partridge in a pear tree.

On the second day of Christmas,
My true love sent to me
Two turtle doves, and
A partridge in a pear tree.

On the third day of Christmas,
My true love sent to me
Three French hens,
Two turtle doves, and
A partridge in a pear tree.

On the fourth day of Christmas,
My true love sent to me
Four calling birds,
Three French hens,
Two turtle doves, and
A partridge in a pear tree.

On the fifth day of Christmas,
My true love sent to me
Five gold rings,
Four calling birds,
Three French hens,
Two turtle doves, and
A partridge in a pear tree.

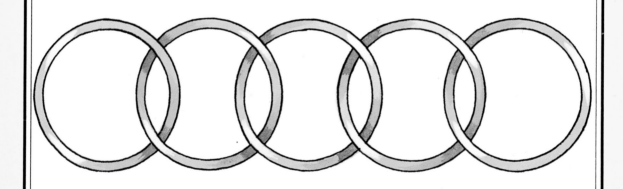

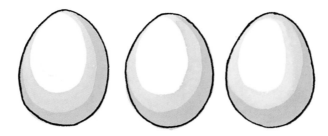

On the sixth day of Christmas,
My true love sent to me
Six geese a-laying,
Five gold rings,
Four calling birds,
Three French hens,
Two turtle doves, and
A partridge in a pear tree.

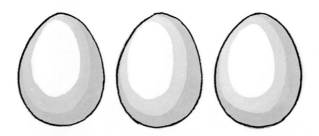

On the seventh day of Christmas,
My true love sent to me
Seven swans a-swimming,
Six geese a-laying,
Five gold rings,
Four calling birds,
Three French hens,
Two turtle doves, and
A partridge in a pear tree.

On the eighth day of Christmas,
My true love sent to me
Eight maids a-milking,
Seven swans a-swimming,
Six geese a-laying,
Five gold rings,
Four calling birds,
Three French hens,
Two turtle doves, and
A partridge in a pear tree.

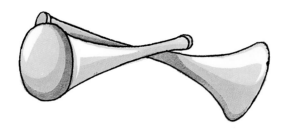

On the ninth day of Christmas,
My true love sent to me
Nine pipers piping,
Eight maids a-milking,
Seven swans a-swimming,
Six geese a-laying,
Five gold rings,
Four calling birds,
Three French hens,
Two turtle doves, and
A partridge in a pear tree.

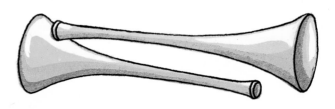

On the tenth day of Christmas,
My true love sent to me
Ten drummers drumming,
Nine pipers piping,
Eight maids a-milking,
Seven swans a-swimming,
Six geese a-laying,
Five gold rings,
Four calling birds,
Three French hens,
Two turtle doves, and
A partridge in a pear tree.

On the eleventh day of Christmas,
My true love sent to me
Eleven lords a-leaping,
Ten drummers drumming,
Nine pipers piping,
Eight maids a-milking,
Seven swans a-swimming,
Six geese a-laying,
Five gold rings,
Four calling birds,
Three French hens,
Two turtle doves, and
A partridge in a pear tree.

On the twelfth day of Christmas,
My true love sent to me
Twelve ladies dancing,
Eleven lords a-leaping,
Ten drummers drumming,
Nine pipers piping,
Eight maids a-milking,
Seven swans a-swimming,
Six geese a-laying,
Five gold rings,
Four calling birds,
Three French hens,
Two turtle doves, and
A partridge in a pear tree.

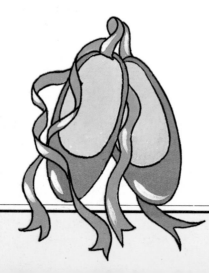

DATE DUE

DEC 13 '89			
OCT 13 '90			
MAY 13 '92			
JUL 2 '92			
JUL 10 '92			
JAN 5 '93			
NOV 29 '93			
JUL 5 '96			
29 DEC 1998			
22 JUL 1999			
GAYLORD			PRINTED IN U.S.A.